THE HORSESHOES OF OAKHAM CASTLE

★ ★ ★

by
T. H. McK. Clough
Curator of the Rutland County Museum

Rutland County Council
1999

Fig. 1. The east wall of the twelfth century Great Hall of Oakham Castle, showing some of the horseshoes forfeited by the nobility of the British Isles to the lord of the manor of Oakham.

Fig. 2. Baron Churchill, coronet with cap and tassel, 1886 (130).

FOREWORD

The tradition that any peer of the realm passing through Oakham should present a horseshoe to the Lord of the Manor is a unique custom, and one that I feel should be maintained and promoted in the present time as a link with our historical past. It is very easy to get carried along in the bustle of the present century, and to forget about our heritage. Oakham Castle is a wonderful link with our past as its walls are literally covered with history.

This booklet gives a detailed explanation as to the origins of the custom of presenting a horseshoe to the Lord of the Manor, and shows how it has been passed down through the centuries. I feel very honoured to be the present Lord of the Manor of Oakham and to enjoy this unique privilege, and hope that it may continue as a custom for many years to come.

E. R. Hanbury
Burley
Rutland

The Lord of the Caſtle and Mannour of Okeham for the time being, claims by preſcription a Franchiſe or Royalty very rare, and of ſingular note ; *viz.* That the firſt time that any Peer of this Kingdom ſhall happen to paſs through the Precincts of this Lordſhip, he ſhall forfeit, as a Homage , a Shoe from the Horſe, whereon he rideth, unleſs he redeem it with mony. The true Original of which cuſtome I have not been able on my utmoſt endeavour, to diſcover. But that ſuch is, and time out of mind hath been, the Uſage, appears by ſeveral Monumental Horſeſhoes, (ſome gilded and of curious Workmanſhip) nail'd upon the Caſtle Hall Door.

Some of which Horſeſhoes are ſtampt with the names of thoſe Lords who gave 'em, with the times when given, as follows ;

Fig. 3.

Extract from J. Wright, History and Antiquities of the County of Rutland *(1684), page 104.*

THE HORSESHOES OF OAKHAM CASTLE

For some four hundred years the horseshoe custom described by James Wright in his *History and Antiquities of the County of Rutland*, published in 1684 (fig. 3), has attracted antiquarian interest. For example, the various English editions of William Camden's *Britannia*, first published in Latin in 1586, when speaking of "the crackt and decaying walls of an old Castle at Oakham", mention "the great horse shoes ... fastned upon the gate and in the hall". Similarly, John Speed, whose *Theatre of the Empire of Great Britaine* first appeared in 1610, remarks that "there are many horseshoes nayled upon the Shire Hall doore, some of large size and ancient fashion, others new and of the present nobility whose names are thereupon stamped ...". Speed goes on to list fourteen named horseshoes, perhaps the first such list to be published. Of these, seven survive today on a board facing the entrance door. Speed also says that there were many others which apparently bore no name.

★ ★ ★

TRADITION: TRUE OR FALSE?

The origins of the custom, which is unique to Oakham, are just as elusive today as they were to James Wright and his fellow historians, who could only write of it as established "time out of mind". By what right or warrant, if any, the Lord of the Manor of Oakham requires every peer of the realm, no matter what his rank, to pay the forfeit of a horseshoe on his first visit, or to compound for it in money, has not been discovered in any documentary sources. The earliest recorded reference to the custom appears to be in a survey of the lordship or manor of Oakham, made for an enquiry into the lands and property of Edward Stafford, Duke of Buckingham, following his execution for treason by Henry VIII in 1521. Here it is said that:

> "there oweth no nobleman to pass through the said lordship [of Oakham], but if [=unless] he do homage to the castle there in giving an horse shoe, insomuch that many horse shoes be set upon the hall door, some marvelous great and some little, with arms and cognizances; and in the midst of the over end of the hall is an horse shoe with the arms of England, being nigh in breadth a yard, which was commanded thither by King Edward the 4th."

(*Letters and Papers of Henry VIII,* III. i, 510-1).

The troubled reign of Edward IV lasted from 1461 to 1483, and so this reference shows that the tradition was certainly in existence by the late fifteenth century. The King's great horseshoe still hangs in the castle (1a).

It is maintained by many writers, more on the strength of tradition than of firm evidence, that the custom originated in the mid-twelfth century, at or about the time that the lordship of Oakham was granted to the Ferrers family. Some authorities have attributed this to Henry II, but the lack of documentary evidence makes this impossible to prove. At Oakham the Ferrers were sub-tenants of the Earls of Warwick in the early twelfth century, and although they were holding the manor direct from the Crown by 1166, it is uncertain when it was granted to them.

The Ferrers were descended from Henry de Ferrers, lord of Ferrières in Normandy, who came to England either with William I at the Conquest in 1066 or soon afterwards. The family name is derived from that of their Normandy home, where earthworks marking the site of their castle still survive. The lords of Ferrières enjoyed considerable prestige, as the senior of six *barons fossiers*, under whose jurisdiction lay the important iron-working industry of the area. It may therefore be no coincidence that the Ferrers were granted land in a part of England so rich in iron deposits as Rutland is. The name is also virtually the same as the Latin or Norman French words for a smith, the *farrier* or shoeing smith of today. Tradition therefore links the custom with a play on the name of Ferrers, something which would be quite in keeping with an eleventh or twelfth century date for its origins. Many heraldic devices contain a punning reference to the names of those they represent; for example, the arms of Ferrers, Earls of Derby, were shown as *argent six horseshoes sable* (six black horseshoes on a silver ground). Unfortunately there seems to be virtually no evidence for the appearance of these armorial bearings at an appropriately early date in the heraldic history of the Ferrers, but in view of the historical background, such an association is not surprising.

The Ferrers were as influential in England as they were in Normandy. Henry was one of the Domesday commissioners appointed by William I in 1086; from him also were descended the Earls of Derby. When his great-grandson Walchelin set about the building of the great hall of Oakham Castle in 1180-90 he was evidently able to secure the services of the country's leading masons. When Normandy was lost to the English crown in 1205, Henry the elder son of Walchelin forfeited his English lands, including Oakham. Upon this forfeiture and the death of his younger brother in the same year, the manor of Oakham was granted to their eldest sister Isabella, wife of Roger de Mortimer, and she held it until her death in 1252, when it reverted to the crown. Thereafter there was no further association between the Ferrers family and Oakham, and it is therefore a curious survival that the inquisition of 1521 should describe the Duke of Buckingham's Rutland lands as being of the inheritance of Lord Ferrers in Oakham. One cannot but wonder what earlier manuscripts were available to the commissioners who carried out this enquiry, which may have contained more detailed information than they recorded, or whether this turn of phrase is no more than a legal fossil.

The various tolls, payments and levies received by successive lords of the manor of Oakham or their bailiffs, together with their other rights, are set out in a number of inquisitions or enquiries which survive from the thirteenth century onwards. None of these earlier records makes any mention of the forfeiture of horseshoes, and there is no suggestion that any comparable toll had been levied elsewhere amongst the extensive property either of the Oakham branch of the Ferrers family or of the Earls of Derby. C. H. Hartshorne, who was unaware of the contents of the 1521 inquisition, expressed great reservations about the possibility of the custom originating as early as the twelfth century (*Archaeological Journal* V, 1848; *Leicestershire & Rutland Notes & Queries* II, 1891-3). He pointed out that the bailiffs of Oakham in the time of Henry III and Edward I (i.e. throughout the thirteenth century) are known to have levied a toll or fine on the passage of carriages, and on the buying and selling of horses and other merchandise. Accordingly, he suggested that the horseshoe toll, which could be compounded for in money, was a natural development from this levy. In other words, the original payment would have been in money, which came to be compounded for in horseshoes. This suggestion gains some support from the fact that in later years the horseshoe fines are known to have been received by the clerk of the market, the official responsible for collecting such tolls; and, according to at least one writer (Moll, *System of Geography*, 1701, as quoted in *Notes and Queries*, 4th series, i, 146), if any peer refuses to pay the toll, "the Bailiff has power to stop his coach and take one off his Horse's Foot". Indeed, the name of one nineteenth century bailiff appears on the horseshoe given by the 2nd Baron Aveland (111). On the other hand, neither Hartshorne nor any other authority can offer any suggestion as to how or why the toll may have come to be levied only from the peerage. It is very different in character from annual rents which could be paid in kind (e.g. a rent of 4d or two horseshoes) and which are frequently recorded in medieval documents. Exactly what happened if a total refusal was encountered is not clear; one writer in *Notes and Queries* (4th series, i, 282), records that two spiritual peers (i.e. bishops) declined, offering an equivalent fee to an unspecified local charity. According to Speed, writing in 1610, the lord of the manor, Lord Harington, was then suing the Earl of Lincoln for refusing to pay the forfeit, an event which might have shed some light on the matter, but the result of the case, if it ever came to judgement, is not known – certainly no horseshoe from that earl survives.

The surviving sources are therefore insufficient to enable one to put forward any conclusive statement about the beginnings of the horseshoe custom. It was undoubtedly established by the late fifteenth century, but even then its origins may have been unknown. It seems that either one must accept a proposal such as Hartshorne's that in some way the custom developed from the normal levying of market fees and dues which was operated throughout the country, or one must accept the word of tradition that its origins lie in the twelfth century. The fact that surviving medieval documents may be silent on the matter cannot be taken to indicate that the toll was not already being levied when the Ferrers held the manor in Norman times. It remains a unique manorial privilege.

★ ★ ★

EDWARD IV

It is specifically stated in the 1521 inquisition that "an horse shoe, with the arms of England, being nigh in breadth a yard," was put up at the command of Edward IV (1461-83). It seems certain that the horseshoe which he contributed is the large and elaborately wrought, though unnamed, horseshoe which still hangs on the west wall (the "over end") of the hall (fig. 4). Although Speed makes special mention of this horseshoe, neither he nor Camden identifies its donor. Its attribution to Elizabeth I by some late eighteenth and early nineteenth century sources must be abandoned as a romantic fiction, and there is nothing to suggest she ever came to Oakham.

It was only when the horseshoes were taken down for conservation in 1980 that it was realised how carefully wrought and decorated this one was. The shoe itself is an excellent example of the blacksmith's art, and its painted decoration, consisting as can now be seen of a row of neatly painted formal roses outlined in black on a red background, must have been most effective. Two quarters of the surrounding shield were painted red, and although no device can now be seen, it seems right to assume that the royal arms were originally depicted on it. Most interestingly, it also bears a stamped name on the left calkin, which unfortunately cannot be read completely, but appears to be "///MOND". This is probably the name of the blacksmith who made it.

The placing of this horseshoe in Oakham Castle by Edward IV can be explained in historical terms. Although Rutland was by no means the principal field over which the Wars of the Roses were fought, one episode of the struggles which took place in his reign stands out as being of more than local importance. This was the battle of Empingham, or Losecoat Field, in 1470, when the King, having marched hurriedly to Stamford, swiftly

Fig. 4. The great wrought-iron horseshoe put up by command of Edward IV in about 1470; and a detail of the left calkin, showing the probable maker's stamp.

scattered an army of rebels from Lincolnshire with his artillery. The mustering of these rebels had been led by Sir Robert Welles, amongst others, and was evidently supported by the Duke of Clarence and the Earl of Warwick (the Kingmaker). After such an apparently resounding victory it would be a suitably royal gesture to put up a horseshoe in Oakham Castle, not in acknowledgement of a service due to the lord of the manor (then Anne de Neville, widow of Humphrey, Duke of Buckingham), but as a symbol or reminder of the King's authority – particularly as the Earl of Warwick's lands, which were confiscated shortly afterwards, included Uppingham, Preston and other Rutland manors. Ironically, the victory was not as complete as Edward thought, and before the year was out, Warwick had succeeded in restoring Henry VI, deposed some ten years earlier, to a brief and shaky rule of a few months.

★ ★ ★

PRINTED SOURCES AND DESCRIPTIONS

Many of the earliest surviving horseshoes, which date from the late sixteenth and early seventeenth centuries, are now extremely difficult to read, and a few are always likely to remain illegible. However, by using the lists provided by Speed (1610) and Wright (1684), some of those which were once thought to be lost or which had been mis-read have now been re-identified. In the case of missing horseshoes whose dates of presentation are not recorded, one can only give the dates during which the donor held the relevant title. Of the fourteen horseshoes listed by Speed, only seven now survive, but their donors have been identified with some certainty from the information which Speed supplied. The same applies to the list of fifteen horseshoes, arranged approximately in chronological order, which Wright gives after his description of the horseshoe custom, and of which again only seven survive. Speed implies that it was only in the latter half of the sixteenth century that it became normal practice to inscribe the horseshoes with the donor's name, and that most, if not all, of the earlier shoes carried no inscription. However, we learn from the 1521 inquisition that it was normal for them to be decorated with the "arms and cognizances" (the crests or devices) of their donors.

In agreement with the 1521 account, Wright's illustration of Oakham Castle clearly shows some of the horseshoes fixed to the door. The doorway was then still in its original position at the eastern end of the wall whose centre it now occupies. There is a similar view in a well-known engraving by S. & N. Buck dated 1730 (fig. 5), of which a very poor copy by Hawkins was published by H. Boswell in 1786; it shows that horseshoes were also placed

Fig. 5. Detail of S. and N. Buck's engraving of Oakham Castle, 1730, showing horseshoes fixed to the door.

on the wooden main gates at the head of Castle Lane, where today there is a pair of late nineteenth century wrought iron gates.

A more detailed account in the *Gentleman's Magazine* for 1796 reads as follows: "According to the liberality of the nobleman who incurs the forfeit, a shoe is made in size, gilt, decorated, and inscribed with his title and the date when compounded for, which is placed in the castle or on the gate, in a conspicuous point of view. Five, and sometimes ten, guineas are the douceur upon these occasions, which the clerk of the market informed me the Earl of Winchelsea, lord of the manor, permits him to have for a perquisite ... Many are gone, for I find the late clerk of the market used to take down several old ones when a new one was fixed, which he gave in exchange to save himself expense. The gentleman who now holds the office rescued a number [eight are listed] from the hands of a smith, which he caused to be fixed against the jury box within the castle." There follow details of 38 horseshoes, including some of those mentioned by Speed and Wright. All but one of them can now be identified, in spite of considerable inaccuracies in the readings given. They include what appears to be the earliest exactly dated horseshoe to survive, given by Thomas, Baron Berners, in 1584.

The "douceur" had certainly increased over the years. Nathaniel Spencer, in *The Complete English Traveller* (1771), says that "it is usual for the peer to give them a guinea or what he thinks proper". This is confirmed in a manuscript source, the Oakham Manor Court rolls. An entry for 1756 (recording an otherwise unknown horseshoe) (45a) reads as follows:

> "The Jurors for Oakham ... do find ... that the Right Honourable John Lord Monson did ... make his first appearance within the Manor of Oakham ... delivering one of his Horse Shoes to be fixed upon the Castle gate there and for a ransom thereof paid one guinea ... "

Other sources contain no original material of any consequence, but sometimes they repeat the essence of the earlier accounts in a most imaginative way. William White's *History, Gazetteer, and Directory of Leicestershire and Rutland* (1846), unashamedly lifting a passage almost word for word from the Rutland section of Laird's *Beauties of England and Wales* (1813), gives the following: "The custom is still preserved, but has long been compounded for in money, as a kind of fee to the *bailiff*, who takes care to be provided with shoes of different sizes, in proportion to the generosity of the donor. Of the horseshoes now in existence, only a few are more than 200 years old, but there is among them every variety in size, from the dimensions of a breakfast table to the measure of a 'Brobdignagian palfrey'." This last astonishing phrase is borrowed from Jonathan Swift's *Gulliver's Travels* (1726).

One other account treats the subject perhaps less seriously than it deserves (*Leicestershire and Rutland Notes and Queries* I, 1889-91) with a reference to the "very elaborate and historical character" of the horseshoes, and an editorial footnote to the effect that "the present custodian of the Castle is not the least among the curiosities shown". Visitors may judge for themselves whether that still applies. Matkin's *Oakham Almanack* for 1892 records that visitors to the town who wished to view the castle should apply to Mr. Edward Smith of the Market Place. He was succeeded as keeper of the castle in 1895 by J. H. Smith, who compiled a manuscript list of the horseshoes in a notebook, dated 1896, which is now in the Rutland County Museum.

Sir John Evans, doyen of nineteenth century antiquarians and at the time President of the Society of Antiquaries of London, read a short paper on the subject to the Society in 1892 (*Proceedings of the Society of Antiquaries*). He notes that "from time to time it would appear that a horseshoe escapes from the custody of the bailiff of the manor, and one that has in some manner become detached from the castle was formerly in the Leverian Museum". That collection, principally famed for its natural history specimens and formed in the late eighteenth century by Sir Ashton Lever, met an unhappy end. The museum proved too expensive to run, and was sold by lottery in 1786 (tickets one guinea) and again by auction in 1806 by James Parkinson whose wife had bought the winning lottery ticket (*Country Life*, 10th March 1960, 494-5). Evans went on to exhibit another horseshoe to the Society of Antiquaries, identified as one contributed by the Bishop of Peterborough in 1693. This one has found its way into the British Museum (38), but the other is lost. Another horseshoe which has become "detached from the castle", but has not travelled very far, now adorns the gable-end of a house adjoining Castle Lane, facing the market place; it carries no inscription.

The horseshoes have been re-arranged several times, for example in 1911 when the castle was thoroughly restored as a memorial to G. H. Finch M.P., and again in 1980 in preparation for the Castle's 800th anniversary. The lists compiled by J. H. Smith in 1896 and by Pearl Finch in her *Oakham Castle* (1903) are therefore useful check-lists, although they contain many errors and are now out of date. It is also known that a number of horseshoes, which had been lying discarded in a corner for some time and most of which were uninscribed, or thought to be so, were disposed of for scrap in the Second World War.

★ ★ ★

Fig. 6a. John, Earl of Exeter, 1714 (40).

Fig. 6b. John, Earl Brownlow, 1818 (70).

THE MAKING OF THE HORSESHOES

Some of the unnamed horses which survive show that the requirements of the forfeit could be followed literally, an actual horseshoe being handed over in lieu of the fine. To begin with, this was probably always the case. By the end of the sixteenth century it had become the practice to hand over, or to commission, a specially made horseshoe, suitably inscribed with the donor's name and the date of his act of homage. Some of these horseshoes, which were often made by a local smith at the behest of the clerk of the market, were not much larger than an ordinary horseshoe. At first they were forged in the same way, with calkins properly formed at the heel, often with a double fullering (with or without nail-holes) and broad enough to carry an inscription. The tendency was then for these ceremonial horseshoes to become larger and more elaborate – although none of them is as impressive as that here attributed to Edward IV. The larger ones may be made of two lengths of iron forged together.

The implication of the 1521 inquisition is that their donors were identifiable by their arms and cognizances, but no such identification survives; it is possible that they were painted on wooden or parchment labels which were lost at an early date. The earliest surviving inscriptions of the seventeenth or early eighteenth centuries are punched, and they are often more legible today than those of the later eighteenth and earlier nineteenth centuries (fig. 6a). A few (e.g. 35, 36) have letters or symbols stamped on the calkins, which may be the maker's or bailiff's initials or mark. The diarist John Evelyn, who visited Oakham in 1654, noted that several of the horseshoes were gilded, a feature which none of the early examples now retains. During the later period the horseshoes were made of thin iron strips with their edges and feet rolled over a wire, or formed of shaped rods, to give them some rigidity (fig. 6b). The inscriptions on these were always painted on a gilded or yellow background, and because the paint has flaked away, faded, and suffered from rust damage, in many cases they can be read only with difficulty Some have certainly been repainted in the past, possibly with different names – calling to mind the practice of re-using horseshoes mentioned in the *Gentleman's Magazine* article of 1796 already cited. Coronets are sometimes represented in this period, but not earlier; where they appear they are made of sheet metal and riveted into place. At least three of the early nineteenth century horseshoes (73-75) are stamped with the name of John Taylor, who made them.

The Duke of York and Albany's horseshoe (58), now very drab, must have presented a fine spectacle. On a gold background there were once detailed leaf patterns around all the lettering, with sequins forming part of the decoration. Its coronet was also finished in gold, with brown, red and black paint picked out with sequins.

Fig. 7a. Rudolph, Earl of Denbigh, 1870 (114).

Fig. 7b. Augustus, Baron Calthorpe, 1898 (141).

The Earl of Pomfret's horseshoe (105) is an unusually decorative one, and is described in the *Stamford Mercury* as "new blue ground, white letters, a border of gold gilt on either side of the edge or rim". Lord Pomfret had been a guest of Lord Aveland at the 1862 Rutland Agricultural Show.

From the late nineteenth century onwards, many of the horseshoes were made in a foundry, a practice which illustrates the growing popularity of cast iron for all types of decorative work (fig. 7). The first cast iron horseshoe, complete with raised lettering, is that given in 1869 by Lord Aveland (111), which was designed locally. Its unusual style is copied on Lord Garvagh's horseshoe (122). There are very many cast iron horseshoes dating from the closing years of the nineteenth century, a period of great activity, and at least some of these were made in Oakham. However, most of the horseshoes made in the earlier twentieth century came from the foundry of S. Russell & Sons Ltd., a firm of Leicester ironfounders, who received their instructions through an Oakham ironmonger (*Foundry Trade Journal* 129 (1970) 662-3). One of the advantages of cast iron was that the lettering and coronet could be formed in the pattern as an integral and permanent part of the design. After casting, the horseshoes were painted or gilded. One of the horseshoes, from Lord Wimborne (134), has a separate coronet, and it is also unusual in giving his motto; another member of the family, the 12th Earl of Lindsey (150), had his made by Robert Benstead, the blacksmith at Uffington, Lincolnshire.

From the mid-twentieth century, most of the horseshoes were once again made by local smiths. Some were made by George Wigginton of Whissendine, others by the Oakham blacksmith George Briggs and his son Richard and, most recently, by Derek Spence of Uppingham. These men hand-forged their horseshoes in the style of the cast iron ones, except that the lettering is painted. The coronets are shown in relief in the same detail, each portion being separately wrought and then riveted and forged into place. Like some of their predecessors, the Briggs stamped their names on the back of the shoes. These horseshoes represent some of the finest craftsmanship of the blacksmith's trade (fig. 13b). A selection of the tools used by these smiths is now in the collections of the Rutland County Museum.

One or two are actual horseshoes with special associations. Mounted on the ceremonial horseshoe given by Elizabeth II (225) there is a racing plate from one of her horses, and that from the Earl of Cavan (188) is a military trophy. Lord Willoughby gave a horseshoe from his horse "Clinker" in 1839 (89); it was stolen in 1846 by an Oakham schoolboy and returned anony-mously together with a piece of doggerel verse, in 1858 when, following his ordination, his conscience would no longer allow him to keep it. The perpetrator of this schoolboy prank has subsequently been identified by J. L. Barber as the Rev. R. N. Jackson (*Rutland Record* 6 (1986) 205-6).

In a typically extravagant gesture, the Prince Regent gave a huge horseshoe decorated with the Prince of Wales feathers and made of bronze (66). The horseshoe given by the 4th Earl of Onslow in 1897 (140) is unique in being made of wood (fig. 9a), but the 7th Earl himself made wooden coronets for the three shoes, including his own, given together in 1999 (236-8) on the occasion of a society wedding in Oakham. The shoe presented by Princess Margaret in 1973 (229) was made of aircraft metal in the workshops of RAF North Luffenham, and that given by the Duke of Gloucester in 1977 (230) is a non-ferrous casting.

In 1979-80, the Castle was redecorated, and all the horseshoes were taken down and conserved at the Rutland County Museum. A few of the least legible were re-lettered, by Russ Thornton of Oakham, to preserve the names of their donors for future generations, before being re-hung, care being taken to ensure this was done with complete accuracy.

★ ★ ★

THE DONORS

The horseshoes in Oakham Castle represent a complete cross-section of the peerage, from royalty and the most ancient and distinguished honours to short-lived or newly created titles. The names of many eminent men can be found – politicians, soldiers, lawyers, diplomatists, churchmen, scholars, landowners, industrialists and businessmen. Some earned their titles in recognition of their services to crown and country, and others lived and worked lives of varying distinction by virtue of the position in society which they inherited.

Many of the honours found on these horseshoes have become extinct or have passed to other branches of the families represented, according to the limitations or remainder imposed on the succession at the creation of each title. Sometimes the continuation of a title has depended on the female line, when a barony has been held by a woman in her own right (*suo jure*). Two such baronesses have given horseshoes, Elizabeth, Baroness Percy in 1771 (51) and Mona, Baroness Beaumont in 1912 (179), and another brought the distinguished barony of Willoughby de Eresby to the Heathcote family by marriage (97, 112) together with the hereditary office of Lord Great Chamberlain.

When a peer is elevated to a higher degree by the creation of an additional title such as an earldom, he continues to hold the existing titles.

One of these may be used as a courtesy title by his eldest son, who may be summoned to Parliament by that title in right of his father. Such courtesy titles are found on the horseshoes from Lord Compton and Lord Hastings in 1621 (24 and 25). Occasionally different titles may be inherited from different branches of the family, to result in a combination of honours of great distinction.

Fig. 8. Walter, Earl of Mar and Kellie, 1903 (157).

This happened in the case of the Earls of Suffolk and Berkshire (167) or the Scottish earldoms of Mar and Kellie (157) (fig. 8). It also occurred with the earldoms of Winchelsea and Nottingham: Daniel Finch, 2nd Earl of Nottingham, who bought the manor of Oakham between 1684 and 1687, succeeded his cousin as 6th Earl of Winchelsea (the senior title) in 1729, and successive earls were lords of the manor for the next hundred years. Another branch of the Finch family held the earldom of Aylesford, and we find horseshoes from the 4th and 5th Earls of Aylesford. Peerages and lands were not necessarily inherited together, and the manor of Oakham then passed to George Finch, of Burley-on-the-Hill, who as MP for Rutland became Father of the House of Commons and was evidently an assiduous collector of horseshoes. Similarly the first Baron Sondes (50) succeeded to the estates but not the title of the 3rd Earl of Rockingham.

Fig. 9a. The wooden horseshoe of William, 4th Earl of Onslow, 1897 (140)

Fig. 9b. Edward, 1st Earl of Gainsborough 1687 (35, centre); Baptist, 3rd Earl, 1694 (39); and Henry, 6th Earl, 1764 (48).

Occasionally the proper succession to a particular title was in dispute, wrongly assumed or wrongly withheld. Thus Sir Thomas Knyvett, by right (*de jure*) according to modern judgement, claimed the barony of Berners (7) but was not granted it before he died and the barony therefore remained dormant until the succession was resolved in 1711. Henry Clifford, son ofthe 4th Earl of Cumberland (18), used the courtesy title of Lord Clifford in the mistaken belief that the barony was vested in his father. The claim of Nicholas Knollys to the earldom of Banbury (29) was never settled.

In addition to Edward IV, two reigning monarchs are known to have given horseshoes, George VI in 1944 when he inspected the Airborne Regiment in Oakham (213) and Elizabeth II in 1967 (225) (fig. 13). Others of the royal family who succeeded to the throne have also given horseshoes: the Prince Regent, later George IV, in 1814 (66); Princess Victoria in 1835 (77); the Prince of Wales, later Edward VIII, in 1895 (137); the Prince of Wales, later Edward VIII (HRH the Duke of Windsor), in 1921 (192) (fig. 11), together with his brother the Duke of York, later George VI (193). Horseshoes from several other members of the royal family will be found in the list, including the Duke of Gloucester (230), the Duke of Kent (231), and the Princess Royal (235).

Horseshoes from local families figure prominently. The most prolific givers of horseshoes are undoubtedly the Cecils and the Noels. The Cecils, as Earls and later Marquises of Exeter, occupy a most distinguished place in English history, and their principal seat remains at Burghley House, Stamford, some twelve miles from Oakham. There are horseshoes from the 6th, 8th, 9th and 10th Earls (the last becoming the first Marquis), and the 2nd, 3rd and 5th Marquises. The Noels have for 350 years been one of Rutland's most influential families. The first of their horseshoes is from the first Baron Noel of Ridlington (22), and there are others from the 1st, 3rd and 6th Earls of Gainsborough in the first creation (fig. 9b). The earldom then became extinct but later was re-created in the same family, and there are horseshoes from the 1st and 3rd Barons Barham and the 2nd, 3rd and 5th Earls of Gainsborough in the second creation, a total of nine horseshoes from the Noel family.

Several other families with strong local connections are also represented, especially the Lowthers (five Earls of Lonsdale gave horseshoes) (fig. 12a), Heathcotes (Barons Aveland, Barons Willoughby de Eresby, and then Earls of Ancaster), Comptons (Earls and later Marquises of Northampton), Spencers (Earls Spencer), Sherards (Earls of Harborough), Brudenells (Earls of Cardigan), and Manners (Earls and then Dukes of Rutland). It is a most interesting exercise to follow the complex patterns of family ties within these dominant families and to see how closely related they were over several generations.

The church is also represented, with horseshoes from five bishops sitting in the House of Lords (three of Peterborough (fig. 12b), one of Ely and one of Carlisle). The 4th Earl of Harborough was rector of Teigh in Rutland for 30 years, a manor which was in the possession of the Sherard family from the early sixteenth century to 1859.

Because Oakham Castle was the scene of the county Assize Court for Rutland, many law lords came as presiding judges, and there are horseshoes from nine Lords Chief Justice (Lords Hardwicke, 1736; Mansfield, 1763, who married the daughter of the lord of the manor; Loughborough, 1782; Denman, 1839 (the third baron gave a shoe in 1906); Campbell, 1858; Coleridge, 1879; Russell, 1900; Goddard, 1950; and Lane, 1981). The last Assizes were held in 1970, and although Crown Courts are occasionally held at Oakham it will only be rarely that a Lord Chief Justice will visit Oakham in the course of duty.

Many other peers who gave horseshoes have had some local association, perhaps in the form of family ties, because they held office as Lord Lieutenant, or were elected to Parliament as Member for the county of Rutland. They may have stayed in Rutland as guests in hunting parties, or may have visited the area on official business. Some of these associations have been noted in the list.

★ ★ ★

THE PROPER FORMS OF THE CORONET

The Table of General Precedence assigns to their proper order below the Sovereign all the officers of the crown, the peerage, clergy, baronetage and people, a list which is long and complicated. Below the Sovereign, precedence is given to the peerage in the following order: dukes, marquises, earls, viscounts, bishops, and barons. The law lords rank as barons unless they are elevated to a higher degree. Within each degree the peers are ranked according to their creation, either of England, Scotland, Great Britain, Ireland, or the United Kingdom and Ireland since the Union. Full details of the Table of Precedence can be found in a standard work such as Debrett's *Peerage and Baronetage*.

Each member of the royal family and of the peerage wears a coronet of an appropriate form (fig. 10). The Sovereign's coronet bears the fleur de lys and cross pattée alternately. Those of other members of the royal family vary according to their status, either as heir apparent (in which case they will also have the feathers which have come to be associated with the Prince of Wales), or a son or grandson of the Sovereign.

a.) The Duke of Leeds (195)

b.) The Marquis of Waterford (152)

c.) The Earl of Londesborough (196)

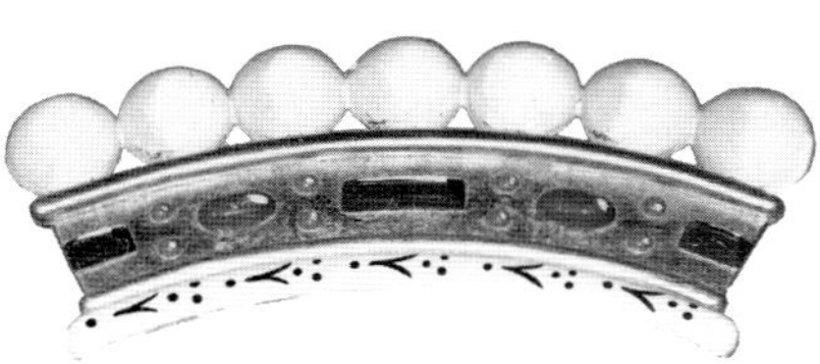

d.) Viscount Greenwood (226)

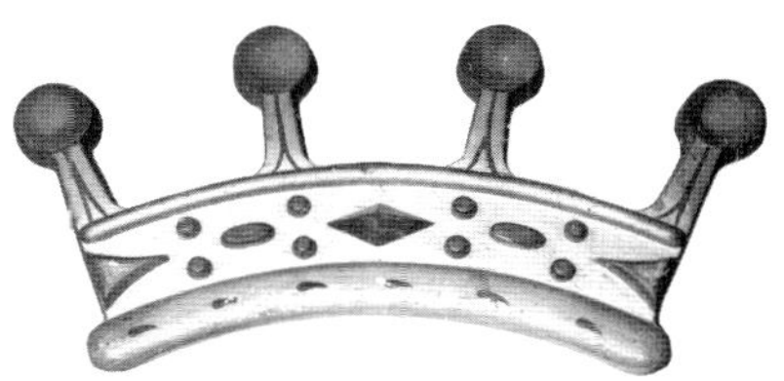

e.) Baron Calthorpe (141)

Fig. 10. Coronets of the degrees of peerage.

The coronet of a duke is decorated with five strawberry leaves, that of a marquis with three strawberry leaves and two silver balls, that of an earl with four strawberry leaves and five silver balls on rays, that of viscount with seven silver balls, and that of a baron with four silver balls. A bishop will normally wear his mitre. Most of the later horseshoes in Oakham Castle are decorated with the appropriate coronet, exceptions being those from the Marquis of Huntly (116), which has the coronet of an earl, and the Earl of Pomfret (105), which has that of a baron. Two other exceptions may be noted: the coronet on Baron Churchill's horseshoe (130) is the only one to show a velvet cap surmounted by a tassel (fig. 2); and the Earl of Darnley's (59) is unique in carrying not a coronet but a helm (the crest is missing).

★ ★ ★

A LIST OF THE HORSESHOES OF OAKHAM CASTLE IN CHRONOLOGICAL ORDER

The list includes horseshoes which do not now survive but which are referred to in the following published sources:

John Speed, *Theatre of the Empire of Great Britaine* (1610).
James Wright, *History and Antiquities of the County of Rutland* (1684).
Gentleman's Magazine (1796); reprinted in *Gentleman's Magazine Library, English Topography* IX (1897); cited as GM.
Pearl Finch, *Oakham Castle* (1903).

Where a precise date is not recorded or cannot be read, a range of date can usually be given, beginning with date of succession to the relevant title and ending with date of death or date of publication as above, whichever is the earlier. Doubtful attributions are indicated as such. Seven horseshoes remain illegible and these are listed first. Normally only the senior title is given, but where another title appears on the horseshoe it is given in the list (e.g. no. 28). No distinction has been made here between peerages of England, Scotland, Ireland or Great Britain. The surname is given in *italics*.

Local associations, dignities and relationships by marriage are noted where a record of them has been found, as these will often explain the presence of a horseshoe from a particular person. The list has been compiled with reference to standard works on the peerage, principally G. E. Cokayne's *The Complete Peerage*. The author is also grateful to R. O. Dennys, Somerset Herald of Arms, for his comments on the completed list.

★ ★ ★

Fig. 11. The Prince of Wales, 1921 (192).

UNIDENTIFIED HORSESHOES

A. Painted horseshoe of early nineteenth century type.
Traces of painted letters visible, but already illegible in 1903 (Finch).

B. Horseshoe of seventeenth century type.
Traces of punched lettering, but illegible.

C. Horseshoe of seventeenth century type.
No lettering visible.

D. Mule shoe.
No lettering visible, but with a punched triangle by each heel.

E. Horseshoe of seventeenth century type.
No lettering visible.

F. Horseshoe of eighteenth century type.
No lettering visible, but traces of red paint.

G. Horseshoe of eighteenth century type.
No lettering visible.

H. Date and whereabouts unknown.
Formerly in the Leverian Museum.

IDENTIFIED HORSESHOES

1a. 1461-83 — Edward IV, King of England.
Very large and elaborately made horseshoe with shield at the top; centre bar decorated with roses outlined in black on a red background, and at the top with a shield quartered in red. Attributed above to Edward IV following the battle of Losecoat Field in 1470, there being no foundation for earlier suggestions that it was given by Elizabeth I.

1. 1544-60 — Henry *Hastings*, 5th Baron Hastings.
Speed, now missing.
Succeeded as 3rd Earl of Huntingdon in 1560. Lord Lieutenant of Rutland 1569-70.

2. 1547-70? — ?William *Willoughby*, 1st Baron Willoughby of Parham.
A very tentative identification, but one which seems possible in view of the family's local ties. The horseshoe appears to read WIL L WIL (i.e. William Lord Willoughby).
An alternative would be William 3rd Baron Willoughby (1612?-17), but the style of the horseshoe makes this less likely.
For the barony, see *The Genealogist* IV (1880) 34ff.

3. after 1558 — Henry *Berkeley*, 7th Baron Berkeley.
Speed, now missing.
Although Speed gives the name as "Bertley" this is almost certainly a printer's error for "Berkley", as no Lord Bertley (or Bertie) named Henry is known. Henry Berkeley succeeded posthumously to the barony at birth in 1534, and was summoned to Parliament in this dignity from 1558-1606.

4. 1569-1605 — George *Clifford*, 3rd Earl of Cumberland.
Speed/GM.

5.	after 1570?	?Charles *Willoughby*, 2nd Baron Willoughby of Parham. Speed. The horseshoe simply reads "Lord Willoughby", but this is a likely attribution. His grandson and heir, William, 3rd Baron, married Frances, daughter of the 4th Earl of Rutland in 1602/03; he himself died in 1610-12.
6.	after 1572	Philip *Wharton*, 3rd Baron Wharton. Speed/GM.
7.	1584	?Sir Thomas *Knyvett, de jure*, 4th Baron Berners. GM. Although GM and Finch attribute this horseshoe to "William Earl Berners", there never was an earldom, only a barony, and no William ever claimed the title. The barony was dormant from 1532-1711 and abeyant from 1693-1711, and so the GM/Finch date of 1704 is impossible. Sir Thomas Knyvett should have succeeded to the title by right in 1581 and did in fact lay claim to it before his death. The horseshoe seems to read simply "Berners 1584", and it can probably be attributed to him In any case it appears to be the earliest dated horseshoe to survive.
8.	1585-1605	Henry *Windsor*, 5th Baron Windsor. Speed, now missing.
9.	after 1585	Edward *Russell*, 3rd Earl of Bedford. Speed, now missing. Possibly a shoe read by Finch and the 1896 MS list as "Edward Lord Aylesford, 1609", which must be a misreading since the title of Aylesford had not then been created.
10.	after 1586	Edward *Sutton or Dudley*, 5th Baron Dudley. Speed/Wright/GM. Finch alone gives the date as 1600. Married Theodocia, daughter of Sir James Harington of Exton, Rutland, in 1581.
11.	after 1587/8	Roger *Manners*, 5th Earl of Rutland. Speed, now missing.
12.	after 1589	William *Compton*, 2nd Baron Compton. Speed, now missing. Later 1st Earl of Northampton.
13.	after 1594	Ralph *Eure*, 3rd Baron Eure. Speed, now missing. Speed describes him as "of Parram" but this appears to be a mistake.
14.	after 1601	William *Herbert*, 3rd Earl of Pembroke. Wright, now missing.
15.	1602	Henry *Mordaunt*, 4th Baron Mordaunt. Speed/Wright/GM.
16.	after 1605	Philip *Herbert*, 1st Earl of Montgomery. Speed/Wright/GM. Later 4th Earl of Pembroke. GM wrongly gives the earldom as Mountmorris.

17.	1607 (27 May)	?Henry *Parker*, 6th Baron Monteagle. Wright/GM. Although the inscription, including the date, appears to be clear enough, the attribution must remain open to doubt, since Henry was born in 1600 and did not succeed to the barony until 1622. He died in 1655.
18.	1607	Henry *Clifford*, Baron Clifford. Wright, now missing. Son and heir of the 4th Earl of Cumberland; Henry used the courtesy title of Lord Clifford, since it was erroneously presumed that the barony of Clifford was vested in his father; he appears to have visited Oakham at the age of 15 or 16.
19.	1607?	Grey *Brydges*, 5th Baron Chandos. Speed. The inscription reads THE L SHONDOSE but the date is not now visible.
20.	1614	Lancelot *Andrews*, Lord Bishop of Ely. Wright, now missing. Preached before James I at Burley House in 1614 and 1616.
21.	1614	Henry *Grey*, 2nd Baron Grey of Groby. GM. Later 1st Earl of Stamford.
22.	1617	Edward *Noel*, 1st Baron Noel of Ridlington, Rutland. Wright, now missing. Succeeded as 2nd Viscount Campden in 1629.
23.	1620	Henry *Hastings*, 5th Earl of Huntingdon. Wright, now missing. Lord Lieutenant of Rutland 1614-42.
24.	1621	Spencer *Compton*, 3rd Baron Compton. Wright. Succeeded as 2nd Earl of Northampton in 1630.
25.	1621	Ferdinando *Hastings*, 8th Baron Hastings. Wright, now missing. Later 6th Earl of Huntingdon.
26.	1621	John *Vaughan*, Baron Vaughan of Mullengar. Wright, now missing. Created a baron in July 1621; later created Earl of Carbery.
27.	1628-66?	?Mildmay *Fane*, 2nd Earl of Westmorland. Only the name of the title can now be read, and this is a very tentative identification. Mildmay was Chief Justice in Eyre of the Rockingham Forest Court in 1629 and 1630, and Lord Lieutenant of Northamptonshire 1660-66, when he died. His other local associations, and the style of the horseshoe, make this suggestion possible. An alternative would be his son Charles, 3rd Earl of Westmorland, 1666-91.

28. 1631 — Thomas *Cromwell*, 4th Baron Cromwell and 1st Viscount Lecale.
Wright.
Later created Earl of Ardglass.
Buried at Tickencote, Rutland, 1653.

29. 1655 — Nicholas *Knollys*, putative 3rd Earl of Banbury.
Wright, now missing.
His claim to the title was never settled.

30. 1664 — "Henry Lord Bryon".
The reading of this horseshoe is clear, but the title of Lord (Bryan) has not been traced at this date.
Finch gives the surname as Percy.

31. 1667 — John *Belasyse*, 1st Baron Belasyse of Worlaby.
Wright.

32. 1667 (30 April) — Robert *Brudenell*, 2nd Earl of Cardigan.
GM.

33. 1680 (29 May) — Edward *Clinton* or *Fiennes*, 5th Earl of Lincoln.
GM.

34. 1687 (8 April) — Thomas *Grey*, 2nd Earl of Stamford.
GM.

35. 1687 (10 April) — Edward *Noel*, 1st Earl of Gainsborough.
GM.
Son and heir of Baptist Noel, 3rd Viscount Campden, Baron Noel of Ridlington, etc. Lord Lieutenant of Rutland 1682-7.
PP and TB on calkins.

36. 1687 (14 Aug) — Edward *Ingram*, 2nd Viscount Irvine or Irwin.
GM.
Finch follows the mistaken GM reading of "Irvine" as "Ipswich".
EG and PP on calkins.

37. 1690 — Francis *North*, 2nd Baron Guilford.
GM.

38. 1693 (20 July) — Richard *Cumberland*, Lord Bishop of Peterborough.
Leics & Rut N & Q III, now in the British Museum.

39. 1694 (17 Dec) — Baptist *Noel*, 3rd Earl of Gainsborough.
GM gives the date, wrongly, as 1604.

40. 1714 (7 Aug) — John *Cecil*, 6th Earl of Exeter.
GM.
Lord Lieutenant of Rutland 1712-15.

41. 1723 (7 Sept) — George *Montague*, 1st Earl of Halifax (2nd creation).
GM wrongly reads "Halifax" as "Hertford" and gives the date as 1703; Finch reads the date correctly but gives the name as "Hereford".

42. 1733 (30 May) — Lewis *Watson*, 2nd Earl of Rockingham.
GM.
R and B on calkins.

43. 1735 (10 April) — Brownlow *Cecil*, 8th Earl of Exeter.
GM.

44.	1736 (6 Aug)	Philip *Yorke*, 1st Earl Hardwicke. GM. Lord Chief Justice and Lord High Chancellor. B on each calkin.
45.	1753	Bennet *Sherard*, 3rd Earl of Harborough. GM.
45a.	1756	John *Monson*, 2nd Baron Monson. Oakham Manor Court Roll; now missing. Elder brother of Lewis Monson, see no. 50.
46.	1757	Brownlow *Cecil*, 9th Earl of Rutland 1751-79. GM. Lord Lieutenant of Exeter.
47.	1763	William *Murray*, 1st Baron Mansfield. GM. Lord Chief Justice, later 1st Earl of Mansfield. Married 6th daughter of Daniel Finch, 7th Earl of Winchelsea, lord of the manor of Oakham.
48.	1764	Henry *Noel*, 6th and last Earl of Gainsborough (first creation). GM. Re-lettered 1980.
49.	1766	Charles *Pratt*, 1st Earl Camden. GM. Re-lettered 1980.
50.	1766	Lewis *Watson*, formerly *Monson*, 1st Baron Sondes. GM. Succeeded to the estates of his first cousin the 3rd Earl of Rockingham. See also no. 45a. Re-lettered 1980.
51.	1771	Elizabeth *Seymour, suo jure* Baroness Percy. GM.
52.	1772	The Reverend Robert *Sherard*, 4th Earl of Harborough. GM, now missing. Rector of Teigh, Rutland, 1743-73.
53.	1779	Heneage *Finch*, 4th Earl of Aylesford. GM.
54.	1782	John Frederick *Sackville*, 3rd Duke of Dorset. GM.
55.	1782	Alexander *Wedderburn*, 1st Baron Loughborough. GM. Lord Chief Justice, later 1st Earl of Rosslyn. Re-lettered 1980.
56.	1783	John *Fane*, 10th Earl of Westmorland. GM. Re-lettered 1980.
57.	1784	George John *Spencer*, 2nd Earl Spencer. GM.

58. 1788 (30 March) HRH Frederick, Duke of York and Albany.
GM.
Second son of George III.

59. 1791 John *Bligh*, 4th Earl of Darnley, Baron Clifton
GM.

60. 1793 (18 Oct) Thomas James *Bulkeley*, 7th and last Viscount Bulkeley.
GM.

61. 1794 (22 March) Henry *Cecil*, 10th Earl of Exeter.
GM.
Later 1st Marquis of Exeter.

62. 1807 (26 March) Augustus Frederick *Fitzgerald*, 3rd Duke of Leinster.

63. 1807 William *Lowther*, 1st Earl of Lonsdale.
MP for Rutland 1796-1802.

63a. 1808 (17 Sept) HRH Ernest *Augustus*, Duke of Cumberland and King of Hanover.
Fifth son of George III.

64. 1809 (25 Oct) Charles *Middleton*,1st Baron Barham, First Lord of the Admiralty.
His daughter Diana succeeded him as Baroness *suo jure* and married Sir Gerald Noel Noel, Baronet, of Exton Park, Rutland; their son Charles Noel Noel was created Baron Noel, Viscount Campden and Earl of Gainsborough (second creation) in 1841.

65. 1811 (11 Nov) Albermarle *Bertie,* 9th Earl of Lindsey

66. 1814 (7 Jan) HRH The Prince Regent.
Eldest son of George III, later King George IV.

67. 1815 Heneage *Finch*, 5th Earl of Aylesford.

68. 1815 Robert *Brudenell*, 6th Earl of Cardigan.

69. 1815 William *Legge*, 4th Earl of Dartmouth.

70. 1818 (28 Aug) John *Cust*, 1st Earl Brownlow.

71. 1822 (5 Jan) Richard William Penn *Curzon-Howe*, 1st Earl Howe.

72. 1827 (15 Nov) Brownlow *Cecil*, 2nd Marquis of Exeter.
Lord Lieutenant of Rutland 1826-67.

73. 1828 (29 March) George *Stanhope*, 5th Earl of Chesterfield.
Married the granddaughter of Charles Manners, 4th Duke of Rutland, in 1830.
I. TAYLOR stamped on reverse of coronet.

74. 1829 George Cecil Weld *Weld-Forester*, 3rd Baron Forester.
I. TAYLOR stamped on reverse of coronet.

75. 1831 (4 March) John Singleton *Copley*, 1st and only Baron Lyndhurst.
Attorney General 1824-6.
I. TAYLOR stamped on reverse of coronet.

76. 1834 George *Gough-Calthorpe*, 3rd Baron Calthorpe.

77. 1835 (21 Sept) HRH Princess Alexandrina Victoria.
Later Queen Victoria.

78. 1835 (21 Sept) HRH Maria Louisa Victoria, Duchess of Kent.
Widowed Princess of Leiningen, married secondly HRH Edward, Duke of Kent, 4th son of George III.

79.	1837 (June)	Hugh *Percy*, Lord Bishop of Carlisle. Younger brother of the 5th Duke of Northumberland.
80.	1838 (Jan)	Arthur *Wellesley*, 1st Duke of Wellington. The Iron Duke (Field Marshal).
81.	1838	George Horatio *Cholmondeley*, 2nd Marquis of Cholmondeley.
82.	1839 (7 Jan)	Charles Noel *Noel*, 3rd Baron Barham. Later 1st Earl of Gainsborough (second creation).
83.	1839 (22 Jan)	Robert *Jocelyn*, 3rd Earl of Roden.
84.	1839 (8 March)	Thomas *Denman*, 1st Baron Denman. Lord Chief Justice of the Queen's Bench.
85.	1839 (12 July)	James *Scarlett*, 1st Baron Abinger Lord Chief Baron of the Exchequer. Contemporary account in the *Stamford Mercury*.
86.	1839 (15 Oct)	Randolph *Stewart*, 9th Earl of Galloway.
87.	1840	George *Davys,* Lord Bishop of Peterborough.
88.	1840	John Charles *Spencer*, 3rd Earl Spencer.
89.	1839	Peter Robert *Drummond-Willoughby*, 22nd Baron Willoughby de Eresby. Joint Hereditary Lord Great Chamberlain. This shoe, from Lord Willoughby's horse "Clinker", was stolen in 1846, as a schoolboy prank, and returned in 1858. The name CLINKER is painted on reverse.
90.	1841	Charles William *Wentworth-Fitzwilliam*, 5th Earl Fitzwilliam.
91.	1845	HRH Adolphus Frederick, Duke of Cambridge. 7th son of George III.
92.	1848	Spencer Joshua Alwyne *Compton*, 2nd Marquis of Northampton.
93.	1852	George *Hay,* 8th Marquis of Tweeddale.
94.	1853 (1 Dec)	Frederick Henry Paul *Methuen*, 2nd Baron Methuen.
95.	1855	William *Edwardes*, 3rd Baron Kensington.
96.	1856	Charles Crespigny *Vivian*, 2nd Baron Vivian.
97.	1856	Gilbert John *Heathcote*, 1st Baron Aveland. Married Baroness Willoughby de Eresby, baroness *suo jure*, so that their son became the 24th Baron Willoughby de Eresby (see 111).
98.	1856	James *Parke*, 1st and only Baron Wensleydale.
99.		See 63a
100.	1858 (5 March)	John *Campbell*, Baron Campbell. Lord Chief Justice of the Queen's Bench, later Lord Chancellor.
101.	1859	Richard Henry Fitzroy *Somerset*, 2nd Baron Raglan.
102.	1861 (25 July)	James *Talbot*, 4th Baron Talbot de Malahide. President of the Archaeological Institute.
103.	1861 (28 Nov)	Adam *Duncan-Haldane*, 2nd Earl Camperdown.
104.	1862	William Thomas Horner *Fox-Strangways*, 4th Earl of Ilchester.

105. 1862 (Dec) George William Richard *Fermor*, 5th and last Earl of Pomfret.
Finch reads "1562".
It has the coronet of a baron.

106. 1864 Granville George *Leveson-Gower*, 2nd Earl Granville.

107. 1866 Somerset Arthur *Butler*, 5th Earl of Carrick.

108. 1867 (28 Nov) William Alleyne *Cecil*, 3rd Marquis of Exeter.

109. 1867 Charles George *Noel*, 2nd Earl of Gainsborough.
Lord Lieutenant of Rutland 1867-81.

110. 1868 John Thomas *Freeman-Mitford*, 2nd and last Baron Redesdale.
Later 1st and only Earl of Redesdale.

111. 1869 Gilbert Henry *Heathcote*, 2nd Baron Aveland.
Later 1st Earl of Ancaster and 24th Lord Willoughby de Eresby, and joint Hereditary Lord Great Chamberlain.
The first cast iron horseshoe – note the raised lettering. DRAWN BY B. T. BRUCE and J. B. BRUCE BAILIFF cast on the face at heels of shoe.

112. 1869 John *Trollope*, 1st Baron Kesteven.

113. 1869 Henry *Fitzalan-Howard*, 15th Duke of Norfolk.
BT (monogram) BRUCE painted on face.

114. 1870 Rudolph William Basil *Feilding*, 8th Earl of Denbigh.
M. WOOTTON E. stamped on reverse.

115. 1871 Fox *Maude*, 11th Earl of Dalhousie.

116. 1871 Charles *Gordon*, 11th Marquis of Huntly.
Premier Marquis in the peerage of Scotland. The horseshoe reads 10th Marquis in error – he died in 1863.
It has the coronet of an earl.

117. 1872 Henry *Lowther*, 3rd Earl of Lonsdale.
J. SHARPE, OAKHAM stamped on reverse of coronet.

118. 1873 (8 Jan) HRH Mary Adelaide Wilhelmina Elizabeth, Duchess of Teck.
Daughter of HRH The Duke of Cambridge 7th son of George III.

119. 1876 Henry James *Stuart Richardson,* 5th Earl Castle Stuart.
Finch reads "Castlehurst".

120. 1877 St George Henry *Lowther*, 4th Earl of Lonsdale.

121. 1879 John Duke *Coleridge*, 1st Baron Coleridge.
Lord Chief Justice.

122. 1880 Charles John Spencer George *Canning*, 3rd Baron Garvagh.

123. 1881 (Jan) HRH Alexandra, Princess of Wales.
Eldest daughter of Christian IX of Denmark.
HRH the PRINCESS OF WALES, NORMANTON WORKS, 13TH JANY 1881 marked with centre pops on reverse.

124. 1882 William John *Tollemache*, 9th Earl of Dysart.
Lord Lieutenant of Rutland 1881-1906.

125. 1882 Charles William Francis *Noel*, 3rd Earl of Gainsborough.
Finch wrongly says this is the first cast iron horseshoe (see 111).

Fig. 12a. Henry, 3rd Earl of Lonsdale, 1872 (117), and Lancelot, 6th Earl of Lonsdale, 1944 (214).

Fig. 12b. Edward, Lord Bishop of Peterborough, 1910 (177).

126. 1884 William John Arthur Charles James *Cavendish-Bentinck*, 6th Duke of Portland.

127. 1885 John Henry de la Poer *Beresford*, 5th Marquis of Waterford.

128. 1885 George Henry Hugh *Cholmondeley*, 4th Marquis of Cholmondeley.

129. 1885 Hugh Cecil *Lowther*, 5th Earl of Lonsdale.

130. 1886 Victor Albert *Spencer*, 3rd Baron Churchill.
Later 1st Viscount Churchill.

131. 1889 George Sholto Gordon *Douglas-Pennant,* 2nd Baron Penrhyn of Llandegai.

132. 1891 William Charles *Evans-Freke*, 8th Baron Carbery.
High Sheriff of Rutland 1862.

133. 1891 Augustus John Henry Beaumont *Paulet*, 15th Marquis of Winchester.

134. 1892 Ivor Bertie *Guest*, 1st Baron Wimborne.
Grandson of Albermarle Bertie, 9th Earl of Lindsey.
His son was created Baron Ashby St Ledgers.
The shoe carries the motto "Ferro non Gladio"; the coronet is separate.

135. 1893 George Devereux de Vere *Capell*, 7th Earl of Essex.

136. 1894 (17 May) Francis Archibald *Douglas*, Viscount Drumlanrig, 1st and only Baron Kelhead.
Eldest son of the 9th Marquis of Queensbury.

137. 1895 (April) HRH Albert Edward, Prince of Wales.
Later King Edward VII.

138. 1895 HRH Arthur William Patrick Albert, Duke of Connaught.
Third son of Queen Victoria.

139. 1895 Charles Richard John *Spencer-Churchill*, 9th Duke of Marlborough.

140. 1897 William Hillier *Onslow*, 4th Earl of Onslow.
Connected by marriage with the Fludyer family of Ayston, Rutland.

141. 1898 Augustus *Gough-Calthorpe*, 6th Baron Calthorpe.
Finch reads "6th Lord Cholmondeley".

142. 1898 Charles Robert *Carrington*, 1st and only Earl Carrington.

143. 1899 William Thomas Brownlow *Cecil*, 5th Marquis of Exeter.

144. 1899 Henry Edward *Fox-Strangways*, 5th Earl of Ilchester.

145. 1898 James Edward William Theobald *Butler*, 3rd Marquis of Ormonde.

146. 1899 Julian *Pauncefote*, 1st and only Baron Pauncefote.

147. 1900 Henry *Hawkins*, 1st and only Baron Brampton.

148. 1900 John Henry *Trollope*, 2nd Baron Kesteven.

149. 1900 Arthur FitzGerald *Kinnaird*, 11th Baron Kinnaird.
Married the granddaughter of Charles Noel Noel, 1st Earl of Gainsborough.

150. 1900 Montagu Peregrine Albermarle *Bertie*, 12th Earl of Lindsey.

151. 1900 Charles *Russell*, Baron Russell of Killowen.
Lord Chief Justice.

152. 1900 Henry de la Poer *Beresford*, 6th Marquis of Waterford.

153. 1901 Henry John *Innes-Ker*, 8th Duke of Roxburghe.

154. 1902 Gavin George *Hamilton*, 2nd Baron Hamilton of Dalzell.

155. 1902 Cromartie *Sutherland-Leveson-Gower*, 4th Duke of Sutherland.

156. 1903 Henry Arthur Mornington *Wellesley*, 3rd Earl Cowley.

157. 1903 Walter John Francis *Erskine*, 14th Earl of Mar and 12th Earl of Kellie.

158. 1903 Charles Henry *Wyndham*, 3rd Baron Leconfield.

159. 1904 Henry de Vere *Vane*, 9th Baron Barnard.

160. 1904 George Henry *Cadogan*, 5th Earl Cadogan.

161. 1904 Charles Compton William *Cavendish*, 3rd Baron Chesham.

162. 1904 Henry *Matthews*, 1st and only Viscount Llandaff.

163. 1904 Charles Stewart *Vane-Tempest-Stewart*, 6th Marquis of Londonderry.

164. 1904 Hugh Richard Arthur *Grosvenor*, 2nd Duke of Westminster.

165. 1905 (26 Oct) Edward *St Leger*, 6th Viscount Doneraile.

166. 1905 Frederick John *Gerard*, 3rd Baron Gerard of Bryn.

167. 1905 Henry Molyneux Paget *Howard*, 19th Earl of Suffolk and 12th Earl of Berkshire.
The last horseshoe recorded by Finch.

168. 1906 Thomas *Denman*, 3rd Baron Denman.

169. 1906 John *Powys*, 5th Baron Lilford.

170. 1907 John *Crichton-Stuart*, 4th Marquis of Bute.
Married the granddaughter of Charles George Noel, 2nd Earl of Gainsborough.

171. 1907 Bernard *Coleridge*, 2nd Baron Coleridge.

172 1907 Philip *Sidney*, 3rd Baron de l'Isle and Dudley.

173. 1908 Edward Lenox *Dutton*, 4th Baron Sherborne.

174. 1909 John Hew North Gustave Henry Hamilton *Dalrymple*, 11th Earl of Stair.

175. 1910 Ivor Churchill *Guest*, 1st Baron Ashby St Ledgers.
Later succeeded as 2nd Baron Wimborne and created 1st Viscount Wimborne.

176. 1910 Henry Alexander Gordon *Howard*, 4th Earl of Effingham.

177. 1911 Edward *Carr-Glyn*, Lord Bishop of Peterborough.

178. 1911 Gilbert *Heathcote*, 1st Earl of Ancaster.
The first Earl of Ancaster actually died in 1910, having provided a horseshoe in 1869 as 2nd Baron Aveland; but it seems more likely that he provided a second shoe to commemorate his earldom than that his son, the second earl, should have given two shoes, one in 1911 and another in 1927 (q.v.).

179. 1912 (3 Dec) Mona *Stapleton, suo jure* Baroness Beaumont.

180. 1913 Adelbert *Cust*, 3rd and last Earl Brownlow.
GREEN. ENG^{R}. H.H. engraved on brass mounting plate.

181. 1914 — Josslyn Francis *Pennington*, 5th and last Baron Muncaster.

182. 1914 — John Henry *Brocklehurst*, 1st and only Baron Ranksborough (of Ranksborough, Rutland).
Lord Lieutenant of Rutland 1906-21.

183. 1914 — Edward *Turnour*, 6th Earl Winterton.
Stolen in 1972.

184. 1916 — Niall *Campbell*, 10th Duke of Argyll.

185. 1916 — Charles Stewart Henry *Vane-Tempest-Stewart*, 7th Marquis of Londonderry.

186. 1917 — John Denton Pinkstone *French*, 1st Viscount French of Ypres.
Later 1st Earl of Ypres.

187. 1917 — Alfred Frederick George Beresford *Lumley*, 10th Earl of Scarbrough.

188. 1918? — Frederick Rudolph *Lambert*, 10th Earl of Cavan.
The shoe is from an Austrian pony captured in Italy in 1918.

189. 1920 — Somerset Frederick *Gough-Calthorpe*, 8th Baron Calthorpe.

190. 1920 — George Henry Robert *Child-Villiers*, 8th Earl of Jersey.

191. 1921 — HRH Victoria Alexandra Alice Mary, The Princess Royal.

192. 1921 — HRH Edward Albert Christian George Andrew Patrick David, Prince of Wales.
Later King Edward VIII, HRH The Duke of Windsor.

193. 1921 — HRH Albert Frederick Arthur George, Duke of York.
Later King George VI (see 215).

194. 1921 — Adelbert Salusbury Cockayne *Cust*, 5th Baron Brownlow.

195. 1921 — George Godolphin *Osborne*, 10th Duke of Leeds.

196. 1921 — Hugo William Cecil *Denison*, 4th and last Earl of Londesborough.

197. 1921 — George Bridges Harley Guest *Rodney*, 8th Baron Rodney.

198. 1922 — Herman Alfred *Stern*, 2nd Baron Michelham.

199. 1925 — Mark Everard *Pepys*, 6th Earl of Cottenham.

200. 1927 — Gilbert *Heathcote-Drummond-Willoughby*, 2nd Earl of Ancaster.
Also 26th Baron Willoughby de Eresby.
Lord Lieutenant of Rutland 1921-51.

201. 1927 — Kenneth FitzGerald *Kinnaird*, 12th Baron Kinnaird.

202. 1927 — Bentley Lionel John *Tollemache*, 3rd Baron Tollemache.

203. 1928 (10 June) — George Charles *Montagu*, 9th Earl of Sandwich.

204. 1930 — Geoffrey William Richard Hugh *Fitz-Clarence*, 5th Earl of Munster.

205. 1930 — Hugh William Osbert *Molyneux*, 7th and last Earl of Sefton.

206. 1930 — Jesse *Boot*, 1st Baron Trent.

207. 1931 — John Campbell *Boot*, 2nd Baron Trent.
G. BRIGGS, OAKHAM stamped on reverse.

208. 1933 — Hugh William *Fortescue*, 5th Earl Fortescue.

Fig. 13a. George VI, cast coronet, 1944 (213).

Fig. 13b. Elizabeth II, hand-forged coronet, 1967 (225).

209. 1933 — Thomas Godfrey Polson *Corbett*, 2nd Baron Rowallan.
G. BRIGGS, OAKHAM stamped on reverse.

210. 1936 — Charles Alfred Euston *FitzRoy*, 10th Duke of Grafton.

211. 1936 — Charles John Haswell *Kemeys-Tynte*, 9th Baron Wharton.

212. 1938 — Reginald Bethune Lindsey *Bethune*, 12th Earl of Lindsey (Lord Lindsey of the Byres).

213. 1944 — His Majesty King George VI.

214. 1944 — Lancelot Edward *Lowther*, 6th Earl of Lonsdale.

215. 1945 — Anthony Gerard Edward *Noel*, 5th Earl of Gainsborough.

216. 1948 — Eric Spencer *Wentworth-Fitzwilliam*, 9th Earl Fitzwilliam.

217. 1950 — Rayner *Goddard*, Baron Goddard.
Lord Chief Justice.

218. 1955 — HRH Prince Henry William Frederick Albert, Duke of Gloucester.
Third son of King George V.

219. 1955 — Denis Anthony Brian *Butler*, 9th Earl of Lanesborough.
G. BRIGGS, OAKHAM stamped on reverse.

220. 1957 — HRH Prince Philip, Duke of Edinburgh.
R. BRIGGS, OAKHAM stamped on reverse.
BILLOWS & SON OAKHAM in pencil (gilding and painting).

221. 1960 — Albert Edward John *Spencer*, 7th Earl Spencer.
Grandfather of Diana, Princess of Wales.

222. 1962 — John Frederic *Gretton*, 2nd Baron Gretton.

223. 1963 (Aug) — Charles John Robert *Manners*, 10th Duke of Rutland.

224. 1965 — Andrew Robert Buxton *Cavendish*, 11th Duke of Devonshire.

225. 1967 — Her Majesty Queen Elizabeth II.
The centre shoe is a racing plate from the Queen's horse, Oriel.

226. 1967 — David Henry Hamar *Greenwood*, 2nd Viscount Greenwood.

227. 1968 — Ivor Fox-Strangways *Guest*, 3rd Viscount Wimborne.

228. 1969 — Jeffery John Archer *Amherst*, 5th Earl Amherst.

229. 1973 — HRH Princess Margaret, Countess of Snowdon.
MANUFACTURED BY STATION WORKSHOPS, ROYAL AIR FORCE, NORTH LUFFENHAM, JUNE 1973 on reverse.

230. 1977 — HRH Prince Richard Alexander Walter George, Duke of Gloucester.

231. 1979 — HRH Prince Edward George Nicholas Paul Patrick, Duke of Kent.

232. 1979 — William Henry *Pilkington*, Baron Pilkington (life peer).

233. 1981 — Geoffrey Dawson *Lane*, Baron Lane (life peer).
Lord Chief Justice of England (1980-92).

234. 1997 — Robert Washington *Shirley*, 13th Earl Ferrers.

235. 1999 — HRH Princess Anne Elizabeth Alice Louise, The Princess Royal.

236. 1999 — Michael William Coplestone Dillon *Onslow*, 7th Earl of Onslow.

237. 1999 — Charles Melville *McLaren*, 3rd Baron Aberconway.

238. 1999 — David Lockhart-Mure *Renton*, Baron Renton (life peer).

Further information
For a description of the building and a historical account, see the companion publication by T. H. McK. Clough, *Oakham Castle: a guide and history* (3rd ed., Rutland County Council 1999).

For details of opening times and other information, please enquire at the Rutland County Museum, Catmose Street, Oakham, Rutland, LE15 6HW.

Photography by Iona Cruickshank, Stephen Thursfield and Richard Adams

Published by Rutland County Council
Catmose, Oakham, Rutland, LE15 6HP

Third edition

First published by Leicestershire Museums, Arts & Records Service for the Friends of the Rutland County Museum 1978
Second edition with corrections 1987

Distributed by Rutland County Museum,
Catmose Street, Oakham, Rutland, LE15 6HW

Printed by deVoyle Litho, Rural Industries, John O'Gaunt, Leicestershire

ISBN 0 9536627 1 3